Contents

Starting a Business
Starting a Business Enterprise 6
Setting Business Aims and Objectives........ 7
Business Planning...........................8
Choosing the Appropriate Legal Structure for the Business 10
Choosing the Location of the Business...................... 12
Starting a Business Test Yourself 14
Starting a Business Practice Questions......................... 15

Marketing
Conducting Market Research with Limited Budgets................ 16
Using the Marketing Mix 18
Marketing Test Yourself 20
Marketing Practice Questions..................... 21

Finance
Finance and Support for a Small Business...................... 22
Financial Terms and Simple Calculations......................... 24
Using Cash Flow 26
Finance Test Yourself 28
Finance Practice Questions..................... 29

People in Businesses
Recruiting 30
Motivating Staff........................ 32
Protecting Staff through Understanding Legislation 34
People in Businesses Test Yourself................ 36
People in Businesses Practice Questions 37

Operations Management
Production Methods for Manufacturing and Providing Services...... 38
Customer Service............................ 40
Operations Management Test Yourself 42
Operations Management Practice Questions..................... 43

Exam Technique 44

Index 46

Starting a Business Enterprise

What do you need to know and understand?
- What a business is
- The reasons for starting a business
- Where business ideas come from
- Sources of business ideas
- The importance of identifying a gap in the market
- Product and market niches
- The advantages and disadvantages of operating as a franchise

What is a business?
A **business** provides **goods** or **services** to people, often in exchange for money.
Products are either goods or services.
A **good** is tangible i.e. you can touch it e.g. cars, tables and pens.
A **service** is intangible i.e. you cannot touch it e.g. teaching and banking.

Can you name a local business that provides goods?
Can you name a local business that provides services?

There are a number of **reasons why businesses are set up**:
- To produce goods for sale
- To supply services for sale
- To distribute products to people
- To meet the needs of society

There is a type of business called a **social enterprise**. These are set up to provide a benefit to society. Any profits made by the enterprise are reinvested into the business.

The Big Issue was set up by Gordon Roddick in 1991. It provides a legal income to homeless people who sell newspapers in town centres. The newspaper campaigns on behalf of socially excluded people.

Can you name a local business that is a social enterprise?

Reasons why an **entrepreneur (a person who sets up a business)** might start a business include:
- Challenge and satisfaction
- To make money
- To be own boss
- Government encouragement

Where do entrepreneurs get their ideas from?
There are a number of **sources of business ideas**. These include:
- Personal experience – daily experience of problems that a new product might solve
- Business experience – from working in a business environment
- Market research – primary and secondary
- Eureka moment – sudden inspiration for a new product
- Brain storming – sharing ideas with others

Mandy Habermann invented the Anywayup Cup after seeing a toddler leave juice stains on a cream coloured carpet – she invented a cup that did not spill by only releasing liquid when a child drank from it.

Many start-up businesses spend time **looking for a gap in the market** and whether that gap needs filling. This might depend upon:
- Trends in the market
- Market research
- Bringing in an idea from abroad
- Meeting a personal need

A **niche** is a gap in the market. Identification of a **product or market niche** is important to see if a need has not yet been met. This may be for a specific type of person, a new product or in a different geographical location.

An entrepreneur can set up an independent business e.g. Sam's Sandwich Shop or trade as a franchise e.g Sam buys the right to trade as a Subway.

A **franchise** is when one business (**the franchisor**) gives another business (**the franchisee**) the right to trade using its name and to sell its products. The franchisee will normally pay a fee and a percentage of its profit to the franchisor.

What are the advantages and disadvantages of trading as a franchise?	
ADVANTAGES	DISADVANTAGES
Lower risk option	Set up and running costs can be high
Already established	Share profit
Recognised brand	Reliant on others
Help and support	Less independence in decision making
National advertising and promotion	Damage to brand reputation if poor quality
Tried and tested business idea	Have to buy products from franchisee

Can you name a local business that trades as a franchise?

Would you prefer to set up a business as an independent firm or a franchise?
Can you justify your decision?

Setting Business Aims and Objectives

What do you need to know and understand?
- Types of business aims and objectives
- The purpose of setting objectives
- How businesses use objectives to measure success
- The importance of stakeholders in influencing the objectives of a small business

What are business aims and objectives?
Business aims and objectives are the goals that a business wants to achieve.
Aims are general e.g. market growth.
Objectives are specific e.g. market growth of 5% in 2 years.

Business objectives will vary from one business to another e.g.
- a new business may want to survive in its first year
- a sandwich shop may want to gain 10% more customers

A business might set different aims for the short, medium and long term. Business aims might include:
- **Survival** - the ability of a business to continue to exist
- **Profit** - to receive more money from sales than the costs of the business
- **Growth** - to expand e.g. through more customers, sales or branches
- **Market share** – increase the percentage of the total market that one particular brand or business owns
- **Customer Satisfaction** – repeat custom, avoiding negative publicity with positive word of mouth
- **Ethical** - to do the morally correct thing, this can help attract customers
- **Sustainable** – minimising the negative impact on the environment e.g. making use of renewable resources, reducing waste and using energy in a more efficient manner

The Balloon Tree, a farm shop near York, has the following aims:
- *"Fewer Food Miles   More Farm Yards"* • *Ensure all produce is top quality*
- *Source everything locally* • *Make the most of home grown produce*

Can you match the aims of The Balloon Tree to the types of aims listed above?

Why set objectives?
Objectives can help in both the day to day running of a business and in measuring its performance.

Purpose of setting objectives
- Setting targets that the business can work towards
- These provide a clear focus for the business
- Measure actual performance against targets
- Objectives may change as the business changes

Using business objectives to measure success

Business Objective	Use in measuring the success of a business
Survival	Has the business enough cash to meet day to day expenses?
Profit	How does the actual profit compare to the target for profit?
Growth	Has the business achieved growth e.g. increased sales or launched a new product?
Market share	What is the business' market share? How does this compare to competitors?
Customer satisfaction	What are customers saying? Is feedback positive? Are there many complaints?
Ethical	Has it kept its promises? Is it guilty of any unethical activities?
Sustainable	Are targets being met e.g. recycling, energy use, reducing waste?

Stakeholders are anyone with an interest in the activities of a business. They can influence the business' objectives. Who are the stakeholders in a business?
- **Internal** – people or groups inside the firm
  - Owners/shareholders • Employees
- **External** – people or groups outside the firm
  - Customers • Local community • Suppliers • Banks • Government

Stakeholder	Influence of stakeholders on business objectives
Owners/shareholders	Want a return on the money they have invested - therefore want the business to make a profit. May influence how profits are spent e.g. are they invested in future growth?
Employees	Want job security, a fair wage and good working conditions - therefore they want the business to survive and grow. They may also want to work for a business that is ethical.
Customers	Want their needs to be met - therefore they want objectives to include customer satisfaction. Many customers also want ethical and environmentally friendly behaviour.
Local community	Want a positive impact e.g. create jobs and support local groups and not a negative impact e.g. damage to environment – therefore profit but environmental and ethical.
Suppliers	Want repeat business and paying – therefore want the business to survive, make a profit and grow. This can also help the supplier achieve their own objectives e.g. make a profit.
Banks	Want to be confident any loans can be repaid – therefore needs the business to survive in the short term and make a profit in the longer term.
Government	Want to support enterprise and new business start-ups because they create jobs and wealth as well as pay taxes - therefore want the business to survive and grow.

Do you influence the objectives of any local businesses or your school?

Business Planning

What do you need to know and understand?
- The role of business planning in setting up a business and raising finance
- The main sections of a business start-up plan
- Uncertainty and risk for start-up businesses
- Actions that can be taken to minimise risk

What is a Business Plan?
"A business plan is a written document that describes a business, its objectives, its strategies, the market it is in and its financial forecasts."
www.businesslink.gov.uk

What is the **purpose of business planning?**

A business plan is used both internally, for use by the firm's management, and externally, by banks and external investors.

What are the benefits of a business plan?
- Help secure investment and raise finance for the business
  - The plan can be shown to banks, friends and family and grant providers
  - Shows the business can work
  - Shows profit and cash flow forecasts
- Estimating costs and revenues
  - Forecast profit or loss
  - Show cash flow forecast
- Identify what problems might arise
  - Can plan for contingencies i.e. what to do if there is a problem
- Provide a sense of direction
  - Better organised
  - Can plan what resources are needed
- Measure performance
  - Allows success to be monitored
  - Where necessary can make improvements

Advice from the Prince's Trust *"The best business plans aren't long and complex; they explain only the most important information – what you want to achieve, how you will get there and the things you need to do along the way. It's best to tackle a business plan in small chunks."*

How do plans help you?
- Revision plans • Essay plans • Holiday plans

The main sections within a business start-up plan

Goods or services to be provided Name • Legal structure Entrepreneur(s) – skills and experience	**Description of the business**
The short, medium and long term goals How will it measure success?	**Aims and objectives**
Summary of market research carried out Key findings e.g. customer data, customers' opinions Analysis of competition	**Research results**
Target market – what are the characteristics of the customer The marketing mix – product, place, price and promotion Future plans e.g. new products	**Marketing**
Number and type of workers to be employed Skills of management and workforce	**HRM**
Location • Production process Suppliers • Targets for output Actions for ensuring quality and meeting customer needs	**Operations**
Sources of finance • Forecast costs and revenues Forecast profit (or loss) over several years Cash flow statement	**Financial information**

Business plans help to reduce **risk** but do not eliminate it. The main risk for a start-up business is failure and the loss of money invested in the business.

Businesses face **uncertainty** because we do not know what will happen in the future.

Why do start-up businesses fail?
- Lack of experience • Over confidence • Lack of finance i.e. poor cash flow
- Inadequate market research • The state of the economy

What can be done to minimise risk?
- Seek guidance - small business advisers, banks, government agencies
- Know the market - there is no substitute for good market research
- Good financial plans - cash flow is vital for a business
- Recruit the right people – with the skills and attitude to support the business
- Have **SMART** objectives - **S**pecific, **M**easureable, **A**chievable, **R**ealistic, **T**ime based

Choosing the Appropriate Legal Structure

What do you need to know and understand?
- Benefits and drawbacks of being a sole trader
- Benefits and drawbacks of being a partnership
- Benefits and drawbacks of being a private limited company
- The consequences of increasing the number of stakeholders

Legal structure refers to the **ownership** of a business.

These two terms are key to understanding legal structure:
Unlimited liability means that the owner(s) is personally responsible for all of the debts of the business. This acts as a safeguard against overspending but could mean that the owner loses their **personal assets.**
Limited liability means that the owner(s) debts are limited to the amount invested in the firm. This allows owners to invest without fear of losing their **personal assets**.

Sole traders
A sole trader is an individual who owns and runs their own business.
- The simplest form of business
- A sole trader has unlimited liability
- They could lose their home and all of their assets to pay off any debts

Sole trader - Benefits	Sole trader - Drawbacks
Cheap and easy to set up	Unlimited liability
Keep all the profits for themself	Hard work
Accounts are private – cannot be seen by competitors	Limited finance available
Own boss making all the decisions	The owner has to do everything or 'buy in' expertise

Partnerships
A partnership is where two or more people run the business.
- Each partner is equally responsible for the debts of the business
- Each partner will take a share of the profits
- Each partner usually shares in the decision making
- 'Sleeping' partners invest in, but do not run, the business
- Set up involves writing a "**deed of partnership**"

Partnership - Benefits	Partnership - Drawbacks
Risks and responsibilities shared	Unlimited liability
Different skills and expertise	Disagreements can occur between partners
Shared finance – each partner invests making it easier to raise finance	If a partner dies, resigns or goes bankrupt the partnership is dissolved i.e. it stops existing
More input and ideas	Each partner can make legally binding decisions - trust

Who would you trust enough to go into partnership with?
Or would you prefer to be a sole trader? *Can you justify your decision?*

Private limited company

A private limited company is owned by shareholders.
- Ltd. after the company name • The shareholders are often family members
- Private limited companies exist in their own right i.e. the owners and the company are separate legal entities
- The company's finances are separate from the owner's personal finances

Shareholders
- Invest money to buy part of (a share in) the business
- They are part owners and receive a share of the profit in the form of **dividends**
- They have limited liability, can only lose the money that they have invested
- Have a say in the running of the business – **a voting right**

Private limited company - Benefits	Private limited company - Drawbacks
Limited liability	More complex to set up – paperwork & registration
Easier to raise finance – sell shares	Accounts are available for anyone to see
More expertise available	Possible loss of control
Separate legal entity	Limited liability may be seen as a risk by suppliers and banks
Continues to exist even when shareholders change	

Private limited companies must be registered (**Incorporated**). They must send to **Companies House**:
- A Memorandum of Association
  - name, registered office and what the company will do
- Articles of Association
  - the rules of running the company
- An annual set of accounts
  - that can be requested by anyone including the competitors!

The Cambridge Satchel Company was set up by Julie Deane and her mother Freda Thomas in 2008. The company produces colourful leather satchels that might look at home in a Harry Potter movie. As with many family run businesses it has private limited company status. This has made it easier for the business to finance expansion. In 2008 it was producing 3 handmade satchels a week. By 2012 turnover had reached £10 million and the company had opened its first store in Covent Garden.

Increasing the number and range of stakeholders will mean that there is likely to be a conflict of interest.
- Who makes the decisions? • Who has invested money?
- What are the stakeholders' objectives?
  - Short term returns or long term growth?

Does the benefit of limited liability outweigh the potential drawback of an increased number of stakeholders? *Can you justify your view?*

Choosing the Location of the Business

What do you need to know and understand?
- Factors influencing where a start-up business is located

One important decision to make when setting up a business is where to locate. There are 7 factors influencing this decision, these are:

1. The availability of raw materials
Raw materials are the physical inputs that go into producing a good or providing a service.
- Some firms have no choice e.g. mining or fishing
- Bulk reducing firms will want to be close to raw materials to reduce costs i.e. the end product is a lot smaller than the raw materials
- Ability to produce quality raw materials e.g. good land for farming or sunshine for growing crops

"In Britain today - two out of three apples harvested are the Cox variety and are homegrown in the countryside of Kent, Sussex, Suffolk, East Anglia and the West Midlands."
Source: http://www.copellafruitjuices.co.uk

Why is Copella located in Suffolk?

2. Transport
The local **infrastructure** will include transport links such as roads, railways, seaports and airports.
- Ease with which goods and services can be distributed from manufacturer to retailers
- May need a national distribution network
- Accessible to customers, could include roads, parking and public transport links
- Can raw materials be delivered on time?

3. Labour
Labour refers to whether there are enough workers, with the right skills, who are willing to work for the business in any given location.
- Need for specialist skills or knowledge
- Wages demanded – in an area of high unemployment wages may be lower reducing costs

What firms are located close to where you live?
Why do you think they chose to locate there?

4. Competition/other businesses
Other businesses in an area may be good if they attract customers to the area or provide support services. Equally it can be bad if it means each business only attracts a few customers.
- High levels of competition may mean it is hard to gain a foothold in the market
- Sometimes competition is good because customers are attracted to an area where they have lots of choice e.g. a shopping centre
- Other businesses may offer services to support the business e.g. banks, office cleaning and distribution

5. Technology
Technology includes forms of communication and information provision through such mediums as the personal computer, the Internet, fax and mobile phones.
- Ability to communicate with customers, suppliers and other stakeholders
- Opportunities to reach a wider target market e.g. internet sales but still need to distribute
- Flexible as working in a virtual market place i.e. over the world wide web
- May reduce the importance of available workers if they can work remotely e.g. from home

6. Proximity to the market
Businesses will consider how close they want to be to their customers.
- A location that has a large footfall helps to attract passing trade
- Bulk gaining firms will want to be close to customers to reduce costs i.e. the end product is a lot bigger than the raw materials
- Convenient for the customer

7. Costs
A start-up business will have limited finance so will have to consider carefully the cost of different locations.
- Popular/busy areas tend to be a lot more expensive e.g. city and town centres and new shopping arcades compared to side streets or out of town locations
- Wage rates vary in different parts of the country depending upon the availability of workers and the cost of living

In 2013 a new £350 million retail and leisure complex was opened in Leeds. Transport to Leeds is excellent and the train station is less than 100 metres away. The new development, Trinity Leeds, is set to lure shoppers away from other areas such as Manchester's Trafford Centre and Sheffield's Meadowhall. Alongside 120 shops one of the new residents is the Everyman Cinema. This is the first Everyman cinema outside of London. With the biggest financial and legal sector outside of London Everyman believes there is plenty of demand for a high quality cinema in Leeds. Although costs will be high there is a lack of competition in Leeds city centre, Vue Cinema being the only main competitor. The O2 Academy has also seen the potential of this location, opening a 6000 seater music venue next door.

What are the main reasons Everyman Cinemas has chosen to locate in Leeds? Can you list them in order of importance?

Starting a Business – Test Yourself

1.1 Starting a Business Enterprise
1. What is a business?
2. With the use of appropriate examples explain the difference between a good and a service.
3. State two sources of business ideas.
4. Explain two benefits of aiming a product range at a gap in the market.
5. State and explain two reasons why someone might want to start-up their own business.
6. What is a social enterprise?
7. What is a franchise?
8. State and explain two advantages of a franchise.
9. State and explain two disadvantages of a franchise.

1.2 Setting Business Aims and Objectives
1. What are business aims and objectives?
2. State two possible business aims for a start-up business.
3. State two possible business aims for a business that has been trading successfully for 3 years.
4. State and explain two benefits of setting business objectives.
5. What are ethical objectives?
6. Explain how business objectives can be used to measure success.
7. State two stakeholders and explain how they can influence business objectives.

1.3 Business Planning
1. What is a business plan?
2. What are the benefits of a business plan?
3. Explain how a business plan might help an entrepreneur to raise finance.
4. List 5 main sections of a business plan.
5. What is the main risk to a start-up business?
6. State and explain two actions a business can take to minimise risk.

1.4 Choosing the Appropriate Legal Structure for the Business
1. State and explain two features of a sole trader.
2. Explain one advantage and one disadvantage of a sole trader.
3. State and explain two features of a partnership.
4. Explain one advantage and one disadvantage of a partnership.
5. State and explain two features of a private limited company.
6. Explain one advantage and one disadvantage of a private limited company.

1.5 Choosing the Location of the Business
1. State and explain four factors influencing start-up location decisions.
2. Explain why choosing an appropriate start-up location is important to business success.

Starting a Business – Practice Questions

Read the item and then answer the questions that follow.
Total for this question: 23 marks

Item

Fudge Fantastic
Austin had always had a sweet tooth and as a child loved spending time at his Grandma's especially when they made her legendary fudge. Austin has just finished studying A-Level Business Studies and now wants to combine his love of food and cooking with his interest in business. His Grandma has said she will give him the family recipe for her fudge. He has seen a lot of chocolate shops open up in the town where he lives but believes that there is a gap in the market for fudge.

Austin has some savings that will help him set up but not enough. He would need to find an additional £12 000 before he could start making his fudge in large enough quantities to sell. He has been to see a business advisor who has offered to help him produce a business plan.

Austin's older brother, Marcus, has been working as a retail manager in a local fashion shop. He is unhappy at work and has suggested to Austin he give up his job and they set up a partnership together. Austin is unsure if he wants his older brother to be involved in the business.

Marcus has moved away from the busy town where they were brought up to a pretty village popular with tourists. If they do decide to work together Austin is keen to locate the business in a busy shopping centre in town. It is possible to hire old fashioned barrow style market stalls in the centre. Marcus thinks a small shop in the village would be better.

1. State and explain one reason why Austin might want to start up his own business. (2 marks)
2. State two objectives that Austin might set in his first year. (2 marks)
3. Austin is wondering whether to accept his brother's suggestion and become a partnership. Explain one advantage and one disadvantage of Austin setting up as a partnership. (4 marks)
4. Explain the benefits to Austin of producing a business plan. (4 marks)
5. Explain one benefit to Austin of aiming his fudge range at a gap in the market. (2 marks)
6. Austin has agreed to set up the business with his brother.
   They are now considering two locations:
   - A market stall within a shopping centre in the town where Austin lives
   - The quiet village where Marcus lives

   Advise Austin and Marcus which is likely to be the best option.
   Give reasons for your advice. (9 marks)

Conducting Market Research with Limited Budgets

What do you need to know and understand?
- Reasons for conducting market research
- The market research methods likely to be used on a limited budget

What is marketing?
The **identifying**, **satisfying** and **revisiting** of customer needs to achieve a profit.
- Customer needs are:
  - Identified by carrying out market research
  - Satisfied by an integrated marketing mix
  - Revisited by on-going research and relevant changes to the marketing mix

What is market research?
Market research is the collection and analysis of data and information to inform a business about its market.
- Market research will help a business to understand:
  - Its customers' needs and wants
  - The competitors' actions and relative strengths or weaknesses
  - The market place i.e. size, spending habits and trends

Why conduct market research?
- To better understand the customers' needs
  - What products do they buy? • Where do they shop?
  - How much are they willing to spend?
  - Would they buy your good or service?
  - What paper do they read? • Do they shop online?

  Helps to inform decisions about the marketing mix

- To identify potential demand
  - What size is the potential market?
  - How much money is spent?
  - What sales can be expected?

  Assess the feasibility of the idea as part of the business plan

Josh March and Dan Lester worked for iPlatform where they developed social applications for Facebook. They believed that businesses faced problems in developing their use of social media through websites such as Facebook and Twitter. Their market research suggested only 35% of questions to big businesses on social media received a response. This led to negative feedback regarding the brand. Josh and Dan realised that nearly all of the big businesses that they looked at were concerned about developing secure and meaningful conversations through social media sites. This applied both externally, with customers, and internally, with staff. They launched Conversocial, a new business dedicated to helping businesses get the most out of social networks. This was about more than just marketing. Through their market research they had realised that social networks had a range of uses e.g. developing customer service. This has led to them developing specialist software for a range of big names such as Tesco, the Carphone Warehouse and Groupon. A single employee can respond to over 1000 Facebook and Twitter comments in an hour by using Conversocial software.

There are two categories of market research:
- **Primary market research** (field research) involves the collection of first hand data that did not exist before. Therefore it is original data
- **Secondary market research** (desk research) is research that has already been undertaken by another organisation and therefore already exists

	Primary	Secondary
Advantages	Specific to the needs of the business Up to date - new information Can be quite cheap e.g. a focus group	Already collected so quick to access May be from an expert source Can provide a lot of information/data
Disadvantages	Time consuming for the entrepreneur Likely to be relatively small scale and therefore lack accuracy Not designed or collected by an expert	General research rather than specific to the business Often have to pay for it - can be expensive Presents past data

A start-up business is likely to have a **limited budget** i.e. they will not have large amounts of money to spend on market research. This will affect the methods available to them.

Market research methods on a limited budget include:

Telephone and other Surveys
A survey is a set of predetermined questions to be answered by the respondent
Normally questions are short and closed and provide respondents with options to choose from
Surveys can be postal, telephone, face-to-face or on-line

Questionnaires
A questionnaire, like a survey, is a set of predetermined questions to be answered by the respondent
It may include open and closed questions, but primarily closed
It is a relatively easy way to collect consumer opinions

Customer/supplier feedback
Listening to the views and opinions of suppliers who may have knowledge of trends in the market
Collecting feedback from customers maybe through reviews, blogs or when registering ownership

Focus Groups
A small group are asked to share opinions about a product in an informal meeting
Good for encouraging open ended responses
Can be linked with being able to touch, see, smell and taste a product

Would you like to take part in a focus group? For which product?

Internet Research
This involves using information that already has been collected and is available on the internet
A wide range of information is freely available and businesses can carry out research independently
Examples include government reports and the census

Using the Marketing Mix

What do you need to know and understand?
- The four elements of the marketing mix
- How to select an appropriate marketing mix for a small business
- The growing importance of ICT in assisting international marketing

What is the marketing mix?
The effective combination of the four key elements of marketing, known as the four Ps:
- Product
- Price
- Promotion
- Place

Product
These are the **goods** and **services** that the firm provides.

For start-up businesses there is a limited amount of money to spend on marketing activities including product development.
- Research and development is expensive
- It may be difficult to source suppliers

It is important to consider:
- What can be done to make the product stand out from others in the market?
- Can the business build a brand name?
- Will shops be willing to stock the product?

Therefore a start-up business is likely to offer a product that:
- Has a low capital investment
- Targets a niche in the market
- Provides a personal service
- Is based on the entrepreneur's area of personal expertise

Small firms often need to take actions to try and increase sales and gain customers. One way of achieving this is through altering or tailoring the product to meet customer needs. This can involve:
- Additional services • Differentiated products
- Tailor made products • Responding to local demographics i.e. the characteristics of the population

A new business may have identified and be trying to fill a gap in the market.

Price
The amount of **money** a customer will have to **pay** for the product being sold or service provided.

The price charged will depend on a number of factors including:
- Market research findings
- Price charged by competitors
- Costs to the business
- The state of the economy i.e. how much money customers have

In a competitive market there is normally a clear relationship between price and demand i.e. the quantity sold.
- As price goes ↑ demand goes ↓
- As price goes ↓ demand goes ↑

If there is a lot of competition in the market it is harder for a business to raise its price as customers might go elsewhere and revenue will fall. If there is a lack of competition the business might have the opportunity to raise its prices and increase revenue.

Promotion

Activities designed to increase awareness, interest and sales of a product. Small businesses will only have a limited budget to spend on promotion and can therefore not afford expensive options such as TV advertising. Appropriate promotion methods include:
- Advertising in local newspapers • using the Internet
- Personal recommendations • business cards

Place

The **location** where a customer will be able to buy a product, it is important that goods and services are easily accessible for the customer.

Advances in ICT mean that businesses can now use **e-commerce** i.e. selling over the Internet to reach more customers. This can allow businesses to sell in **international markets**.

The marketing mix at Kurt Geiger - *Over 500 million pairs of shoes are sold in the UK every year. The market is worth over £5 billion. Kurt Gieger has positioned itself as a high quality product within this market. By concentrating on design they have managed to gain a loyal following for their shoes and are able to charge a premium (high) price. An important element of their success is how they manage to sell their shoes in top department stores around the country alongside their own prestigious shoe shops. To enhance their image they advertise in high end magazines such as Marie Claire.*

What was the last item you bought? How were you influenced by the marketing mix? Can you justify which of the 4Ps was the most important?

Marketing – Test Yourself

2.1 Conducting Market Research with Limited Budgets
1. What is market research?
2. Explain two reasons for conducting market research.
3. Identify and explain three different methods of market research.
4. What is a limited budget?
5. Explain why a start-up business may have a limited budget.
6. Explain why having a limited budget will affect the choice of research methods.

2.2 Using the Marketing Mix
1. What is the marketing mix?
2. Write one sentence to explain each element of the marketing mix.
3. With the use of an example explain how a business could change its product to meet customer needs.
4. Explain the relationship between price and demand.
5. What is a competitive market?
6. How does being in a competitive market affect the price a business can charge?
7. Explain two promotional methods suitable to a small business.
8. Explain why having a limited budget will affect the choice of promotional methods.
9. What is e-commerce?
10. Explain how the use of e-commerce may help a small business:
    a) Reduce costs
    b) Grow
    c) Reach international markets

Marketing – Practice Questions

Read the item and then answer the questions that follow.
Total for this question: 33 marks

Item

Indian Delights
Haadiya is thinking of setting up a business selling handmade Indian sweet and savoury snacks. All of his friends tell him how good his snacks are and that he should sell them. He recently had a stall at a local craft fair and sold out by lunch time.

Haadiya has decided to rent a small industrial kitchen to make his snacks. He is undecided on the best way to market his business and where to sell his snacks. He was thinking about renting stalls at food fairs but is now considering e-commerce. He recently saw an advert for a company called "Graze". They ask customers to subscribe to them and for a set amount per month they send snack boxes direct to the customer each week. Their boxes contain snacks such as nuts, dried fruits and olives. Haadiya thinks this might be a good idea for his business.

Haadiya's mother has suggested he does some market research to decide if his idea is likely to succeed or not. Haadiya, however, is concerned that this will be expensive as he has only a limited amount of money to set up his business.

1. Haadiya has decided to take his mother's advice and do some market research.
    a) Identify two methods of market research. (2 marks)
    b) For each method explain how it could help him assess his chances of success. (4 marks)
    c) Explain why your chosen methods are appropriate to Haadiya, who is on a limited budget. (1 marks)
2. Haadiya wants to charge £3.99 for a small snack box and £6.99 for a large snack box. His friends love his snacks but tell him this is too high. Explain the relationship between price and demand. (4 marks)
3. Explain how Haadiya could benefit from e-commerce. (6 marks)
4. Explain two possible disadvantages to Haadiya of e-commerce. (4 marks)
5. Haadiya has decided to go ahead with setting up Indian Delights. He will start off by attending local food markets at weekends and delivering to local offices during the week. He wants to raise awareness of his new business.
    He has identified two marketing options:
    - 7000 full colour leaflets printed and delivered to his home for £300
    - Advert in the local paper costing £100 per day, the paper sells 10000 copies per day

    Recommend which method Haadiya should use in order to raise awareness. Give reasons for your recommendation. (9 marks)

Finance and Support for a Small Business

What do you need to know and understand?
- The sources of finance available to a small business
- The difficulties a small business may face when attempting to raise funds
- The sources and types of advice available to small businesses

A small business will need **money (finance)** to cover the costs of **starting up** and the **costs of running** the business. Finance can be obtained from a number of sources:

The Bank – 3 options
- Bank loan
  - A set amount of money borrowed that has to be paid back over an agreed period of time
  - Interest has to be paid on the amount borrowed
- Overdraft
  - The ability to withdraw more money from a bank account than you actually have
  - Interest rates are often very high
- Mortgage
  - A long term loan secured against an asset, normally a building

Friends and family
- Terms and conditions can be agreed between you and them
- May be an informal arrangement

Grants
- Financial support given to a business
- Maybe a government initiative or charitable trust

THE BANK — Interest please!

Source of finance	Advantages	Disadvantages
Bank loan	Lump sum Clear terms and conditions May also get support	Interest payments Strict conditions May not be approved
Overdraft	Flexible Can help with short term cash shortages	High interest charges Bank can demand repayment quickly
Mortgage	Potentially large lump sum Regular pre agreed payments	High interest charges Secured against an asset, possible risk
Friends & family	Flexible May be cheap or even free!	Could spoil a relationship May only be a limited amount available
Grants	Often with added support May not need to be repaid	Difficult to obtain

Why is it **difficult** for new businesses to raise finance?
- Lack of experience – banks may be reluctant to lend
- Lack of assets – what can a mortgage be secured against?
- Limited spare cash – personal savings, friends and family
- No previous profits to feedback into the business
- Grants need to be applied for and are not easy to qualify for
- Viewed as high risk

Many new entrepreneurs starting up a business will **lack experience**. They may be an expert in their given area e.g. as a hairdresser or motor mechanic but do they have business knowledge? They will need **help** and **support**.

Sources and types of advice available to small businesses	
High Street Banks	Appropriate sources of finance Completing a business plan (often provide templates) Often free services
Small business advisors	Legal requirements Potential grants May provide expertise on a regional basis
Private firms e.g. consultants, lawyers and accountants	Professional support on a wide range of issues e.g. tax, legal structure, registering a company Will charge for their services
The Government e.g. www.GOV.uk	Information and advice on a wide range of issues from raising finance to employing staff Free service
Charities e.g. the Prince's Trust	Provide advice and support Possible financial support e.g. grants or low cost loans May provide mentors i.e. one to one ongoing support

All of these organisations offer a wide range of expertise and support from drawing up a business plan, marketing, working with suppliers and securing finance to employing staff and growing a business.

> The Government has created a Business Bank that will provide financial support for small to medium sized businesses. Business Secretary Vince Cable said that the government would fund £1 billion and the Bank would seek to attract funding from private financial institutions to the tune of £10 billion. Traditional banks have been criticised for failing to provide enough lending to small businesses and it is hoped that the Business Bank will help to solve this problem.

Financial Terms and Simple Calculations

What do you need to know and understand?
- Financial terms used in business
- How to calculate profit and loss

In business the word money can apply to lots of different things including **price**, **costs**, **revenue** and **profit**. It is therefore important you always use the correct **financial term**.

What is a business' **revenue**? How much does it **earn** from sales?

Price = the amount of money paid by a consumer for a good or service **e.g. a hand car wash is £5.00.**

Sales = the number of items sold **e.g. 24 car washes a day.**

Revenue = the total value of money being earned by the business from sales.

Revenue is calculated as:
    Revenue = number of item sold x price
    e.g. 24 car washes a day x £5.00 = £120.00 sales revenue per day

What are the **costs** of a business?

Costs = the expenses incurred by a business when providing goods or services **e.g. rent of a garage forecourt, buckets, sponges, shampoo and wax.**

Some costs stay the same regardless of output e.g. rent on the garage forecourt, of £35.00 per day, has to be paid whether 1 car is washed or 100 cars. These are called fixed costs.

Some costs will change with the amount of output **e.g. the more cars washed the more shampoo and wax that is used, at £1.10 per car.** These are called variable costs.

Total costs are calculated as:
    Total costs = Fixed cost + (Variable cost per unit x number of units)
    or
    Total cost = Fixed costs + total variable costs
    e.g. £35.00 + (£1.10 x 24 cars) = £35.00 + £26.40 = £61.40

Having considered both sides of the equation i.e. **costs** and **revenues** a business can now consider the **relationship between them**.

How does a business know if it has made a **profit** or a **loss**?

Profit or Loss = the difference between revenue and costs.

If **revenue** is **greater** than **costs** the business has made a profit.

Profit is calculated as:
Revenue – total costs
e.g. Revenue £120.00 – total costs £61.40 = Profit £58.60 per day

If the business opened for 320 days a year total profit would be £58.60 x 320 = £18 752

Remember in the exam you will need a calculator

Relationships between prices, costs, revenues and profits

A business that wants to **increase profit** has two options:
- Increase revenue e.g.
  - change price to sell more
  - improve product or customer service to attract more customers
  - increase promotion, as long as the cost of the promotion isn't higher than the extra revenue gained
- Reduce costs e.g.
  - find cheaper raw materials, but be careful not to affect quality
  - reduce staff hours
  - introduce new technology to reduce costs in the long run
- or a third option – a bit of both!

Rising costs at small businesses - *According to a survey by the Forum of Private Business the majority of small businesses have seen an increase in their business costs in recent years. Rising energy prices have hit 85% of these businesses. Other major increases in costs have come through transport, marketing and the cost of raw materials and stock. A third of these businesses have been unable to pass these higher costs on to consumers in the form of higher prices due to the poor state of the economy. Businesses have also been affected by increased taxes on fuel and bad weather. 59% of small businesses have had trouble with late paying customers whilst 55% have suffered due to competitors offering products below cost. This means that they would make a loss on the products sold.*

Finance

Using Cash Flow

What do you need to know and understand?
- How to interpret a cash flow statement
- The importance of cash flow statements
- The consequence of cash flow problems
- How to identify solutions to cash flow problems

Cash flow is the **movement** of **money in (income/receipts)** and **money out (expenses/payments)** of a business.

Sale of goods
Payment by debtors
Loans received

Raw materials
Expenses
Loan repayments
Equipment

Net Cash Flow
The difference between total cash in and total cash out.
e.g.   Total cash in   =   £2 000
       Total cash out =   £1 400
       Net Cash Flow   =   £600
i.e. £600 more has flowed into the business than has flowed out

Cash flow statements are used to help understand the flow of **cash in** and **cash out** of the business as well as whether the **closing balance** (the balance at the end of a month) will be positive or negative.

Example of a cash flow statement

	Jan (£)	Feb (£)	Mar (£)	Apr (£)	Calculations
Income					
Sales	4 000	4 500	5 500	6 500	
Total income	4 000	4 500	5 500	6 500	Add all incomes together
Expenses					
Materials	800	900	1 000	1 200	
Wages & salaries	1 000	1 000	1 200	1 200	
Other expenses	9 000	450	350	400	
Total expenses	10 800	2 350	2 550	2 800	Add all expenses together
Net cash	(6 800)	2 150	2 950	3 700	Total income − total expenses
Balance bought forward	0	(6 800)	(4 650)	(1 700)	The previous months closing balance
Balance carried forward	(6 800)	(4 650)	(1 700)	2 000	Balance bought forward + net cash

( ) are used to show that a number is negative.

The importance of cash flow forecasts
Businesses normally produce a forecast of their expected cash flow before the start of the year. This allows the business to spot any **potential cash shortfalls** in advance by identifying **negative closing balances**. The business can then either:
- Look to avoid the negative closing balances or
- Make plans e.g. a prearranged overdraft

The business can monitor **actual cash flow** against **predicted cash flow**.

The business can also identify **positive closing balances** to see if too much cash is sat dormant when it could be used to grow the business or earn a higher rate of interest.

Consequences of cash flow problems
Cash shortages can lead to the inability to meet **day to day expenses** e.g. buy stock and pay wages. The business may therefore have to **sell assets** to pay expenses. Failure to cover debts can result in the business going into **receivership** and **closing down**.

Receivership is when an organisation **takes control of all the assets** of a failing business and turns them into cash to try **and pay off the business' debts**. The business ceases to exist.

Solutions to cash flow problems
Reschedule payments i.e. slow down the flow of money going out of the business
- Negotiate credit terms with suppliers e.g. buy now pay in 30 days
- May lose discounts for early payment

Reduce the amount of money flowing out
- Can you reduce costs e.g. find a cheaper supplier
- Might have a negative effect on quality

Reschedule income i.e. speed up the flow of money coming into the business
- Get customers to pay quicker or possibly in advance e.g. pay a deposit
- May lose customers if a competitor is offering credit

Increase the amount of money flowing in
- Take out a loan or attract more customers
- Either option will incur additional costs e.g. interest payments on a loan or need to advertise to attract more customers

---

MarketInvoice was set up to help small businesses access cash from unpaid invoices. The invoices are auctioned, e-Bay style, to larger financial institutions. This provides cash flow to the small business and allows the financial institutions to use their specialist skills to chase up the invoice. Although the small business will not get the full amount of the invoice they will have cash flow to help to pay for the day to day running of the business e.g. wages.

Finance – Test Yourself

3.1 Finance and Support for a Small Business
1. What is a grant?
2. Explain one advantage and one disadvantage of a loan from family or friends.
3. Identify and explain three different methods of finance available from a bank.
4. Explain why a start-up business may find it difficult to raise finance.
5. State two organisations that can support small businesses.
6. For each organisation explain how it can offer support to a small business.

3.2 Financial Terms and Simple Calculations
1. What is meant by the following terms:
    a) Price
    b) Sales
    c) Revenue
    d) Costs
    e) Profit
    f) Loss?
2. What is the formula for total revenue?
3. What is the formula for profit or loss?
4. A business making garden swings has the following monthly financial data:
    - Selling price per swing £95
    - Sales 50 swings
    - Cost of materials £25 per swing
    - Staff and other costs £2 100

    What is the business' profit or loss?

3.3 Using Cash Flow
1. What is a cash flow statement?
2. Explain two possible consequences of cash flow problems.
3. Explain two possible solutions to cash flow problems.
4. Explain the potential relationship between an overdraft and a negative closing balance.

Finance – Practice Questions

Read the item and then answer the questions that follow.
Total for this question: 25 marks

Item

The Hanging Garden
Nancy was shocked to suddenly find herself out of work. The factory she worked at had just announced that it would close. Losing her job was really bad news but she was to receive a £5 000 payment which was at least a bit of good news.

Nancy has always been a keen gardener who loved pottering around in her garden and greenhouse. She started to think about whether she could turn her love for gardening into a small business. Nancy quickly set to work.

Her idea was to invest in a bigger greenhouse where she would grow plants from seed and design hanging baskets. She would then sell these at local markets. She estimated, even with her £5 000 payment, she would still need an additional £4 000 before she would be ready to start trading. This included buying a small second hand van and renting a larger greenhouse.

1. Apart from buying a van and renting a greenhouse state two other costs Nancy is likely to incur. (2 marks)
2. Nancy thinks she could sell 42 hanging baskets at a Sunday market. The average price would be £18. What is Nancy's estimated revenue? (2 marks)
3. Explain what might happen to Nancy's revenue if she lowered her prices to £15. (4 marks)
4. Explain one advantage and one disadvantage to Nancy of borrowing the additional £4 000 from friends or family. (4 marks)
5. Explain one advantage and one disadvantage to Nancy of borrowing the additional £4 000 from a bank. (4 marks)
6. Nancy has just produced a cash flow forecast for the first six months.

	Feb £	Mar £	Apr £	May £	June £	July £
Sales	600	1 800	2 700	3 800	4 800	4 400
Total income	600	1 800	2 700	3 800	4 800	4 400
Expenses						
Van	7 000					
Rent	400	400	400	400	400	400
Materials	210	630	945	1 330	1 680	1 540
Other expenses	1 900	1 200	1 500	1 650	1 600	1 550
Total expenses	9 510	2 230	2 845	3 380	3 680	3 490
Net cash	(8 910)	(430)	(145)	420	1 120	910
Balance b/f	9 000	90	(340)	(485)	(65)	1 055
Balance c/f	90	(340)	(485)	(65)	1 055	1 965

Recommend the best action(s) you would advise Nancy to take in order to manage her cash flow. Use the item and cash flow forecast above to support your recommendation. (9 marks)

Recruiting

What do you need to know and understand?
- The need for recruitment
- The benefits of full-time and part-time employment
- Recruitment methods
- The factors that determine the remuneration paid to workers
- The use of monetary and non-monetary benefits

Recruitment is the process of identifying a vacancy in the workforce and the steps taken to attract the right quality of worker to fill this vacancy.

Why do firms need to recruit?
A firm will recruit new workers for a variety of reasons:
- The business is growing
- To replace an employee who has left
- New skills required
- Increased workload
- Covering positions on a temporary basis

New workers may be:
- **Full-time** – considered to be over 35 hours a week
- **Part-time** – less than 35 hours a week

Benefits of full-time employment	Benefits of part-time employment
Increased security for workers	Greater flexibility
Easier to feel part of a team	Wider pool of workers
Employees may be more committed	Helps keep valued workers within the business
Less people to supervise	Easier to respond to changes in demand
Lower recruitment and training costs	

Recruitment can be:
- **Internal** – appointing an existing employee to a new role
- **External** – appointing an employee from outside of the business

Benefits of internal recruitment	Benefits of external recruitment
Lower recruitment costs	Wider pool of applicants
Greater promotion prospects	Bring fresh ideas to the business
Employees already know the business	More talent to choose from
Abilities of worker is already known to the business	Less chance of resentment

Recruitment methods are how a business attracts applicants to apply for a vacancy. These include:
- **Personal recommendation** – personal contacts e.g. friends can act as a reference for new employees as they have an insight into the skills or integrity of a potential new recruit
- **Internal (personal) recommendation** – a manager might identify an employee for promotion
- **Advertising** – smaller firms will advertise locally to reduce costs e.g. local newspapers, shop window or job centres
- **Interviewing** – this enables the firm to select the best worker for the job. An interview is a two way process. Both the interviewer and interviewee get to meet, work out if they are right for each other and ask questions

Some of the UK's biggest recruiters are using software in order to filter applicants. With online applications it has become easy for firms to use computer programs to look at CVs and decide who to move on to the next phase of recruitment. Using key words early in the CV is important, increasing an applicant's chances of success. Action words such as 'marketing executive', nouns such as 'management' and specific nouns such as 'Microsoft Word' will help candidates through to the next round as businesses sift through thousands of hopefuls.

How would you feel if you applied for a job and your CV was rejected by a computer?

Once an employee has been appointed they are going to want to be paid! **Remuneration** is the money paid or benefits given to a worker in return for their services.

Monetary benefits i.e. pay	Non-monetary benefits
Wages are paid per hour worked	Private health care e.g. BUPA
Salaries are a yearly amount paid per month	Company car
Pension payments i.e. an employer contributes	Fringe benefits e.g. discounts
Bonus for reaching a target	Sports and social facilities

The level of remuneration paid to workers will be determined by a number of factors:
- Level of skills and experience needed for a job
- The number of people with the required skills
- A comparison of pay within the region
- A comparison of pay within the industry
- The state of the economy

High demand for workers or a lower supply of workers will lead to higher wages.

Motivating Staff

What do you need to know and understand?
- The benefits to a business of well-motivated staff
- Methods used by small businesses to motivate staff

Motivation can be defined as the reasons why a person does something.

Businesses will try to motivate workers to meet targets that will benefit the firm. Motivated staff are vital to the success of a small business.

Benefits to a business of motivated staff include:
- Greater commitment from the workforce
  - Staff are more likely to work hard if they enjoy what they are doing
- Increased quantity of output
  - Improvements in the amount of work produced could be a result of greater commitment
- Improved quality of work
  - Higher quality work produced due to a desire to help the business succeed
- A happier workforce
  - People will enjoy turning up for work and there will be lower recruitment costs as less staff leave
- Lower levels of absenteeism
  - Less costs involved in covering for colleagues and lost production
- Less disputes in the workplace
  - Less tension between employees and management will lead to an environment where people can achieve in the workplace
- Higher profits
  - Lower costs and higher output are more likely to lead to a profitable business

In 2012 Shine Communications was voted the "Best Small Company to Work For" by the Sunday Times. 10% of company profit is reinvested into training and a personal development fund allows staff to develop in an area of personal interest such as learning a language. A flexible benefits scheme provides a range of perks such as membership of the Tate Modern. Flexible hours mean that staff finish early on Fridays and are even allowed to play truant on their birthday!

A business may use **financial** and **non-financial** methods to motivate their employees.

There are a number of **financial rewards** that a small business might use to motivate workers. These include:
- **Piece rate** – payment based on the number of items (pieces) produced
- **Commission** – payment based on the number of units sold
- **Performance related pay (PRP)** – a bonus based on the performance of the employee measured against a range of criteria
- **Profit related pay** – a proportion of employee pay varies with the profits of the company
- **Fringe benefits** – non-financial benefits that have a cash value e.g. discount on products sold by the business

All of these methods can motivate staff to work harder but at the same time will increase costs to the business. The business must ensure that the quality of work is not sacrificed.

Every year John Lewis employees look forward to an annual bonus that is dependent on the profit of the business. In recent years this has been as much as 18% of an employee's salary. Employees realise that the greater the profit the bigger the bonus is likely to be. This leads to everyone working together to ensure that the business is run as efficiently and effectively as possible.

A business may also use **non-financial methods** e.g. training and responsibility.

Non-financial method	Benefits	Disadvantages
Training	• Improved skills and knowledge • Feel valued • Aim for promotion • Can often lead to qualifications	• Costs in terms of time and money • If done during work time can lead to a loss of productivity • May leave to work elsewhere
Responsibility	• Sense of achievement • Self esteem i.e. feel good about self and the job • Job enrichment i.e. more interesting and challenging tasks to do • Recognition	• Mistakes may be made which may be costly in a small firm • Tension between workers who are overlooked • May expect higher pay

Would payment by results motivate you to do well in your GCSEs?

Protecting Staff through Understanding Legislation

What do you need to know and understand?
- The legal responsibilities of employers and their staff
- How laws can affect small businesses

Legislation is law passed, mainly through Acts of Parliament. There are a number of laws that are designed to protect the rights of the workforce.

Equal pay and minimum wage laws
These are laws that impact upon the pay of the workforce and therefore the costs of a business.
- Equal Pay
  - Men and women must be paid the same pay for the same job or a job of equal value
- Minimum Wage
  - Firms must pay at least a minimum amount of money per hour
  - The minimum amount depends upon the employee's age and is reviewed by the government each year

> **What are the current minimum wage rates?**
> https://www.gov.uk/national-minimum-wage-rates

Discrimination
These are laws that attempt to stop workers being treated differently (discriminated against).
- Laws exist that state employees can not be discriminated against based on:
  - gender • age • race • religion • sexual orientation • disability
- This relates to every stage of recruitment:
  - advertising the job and selecting the best person for the job
  - pay and treatment at work
  - dismissal

Employment rights
These are laws that attempt to protect all employees by giving them certain entitlements (rights).
- Terms and conditions of employment should be laid out in a contract of employment e.g. holiday entitlement, working hours and disciplinary procedures
- Rights of employees in terms of maternity and paternity leave
- Protecting an employee against unfair dismissal

Employment rights – flexible working hours - *Deputy Prime Minister Nick Clegg has proposed changes to flexible working hours to come into place by 2015. The proposals mean that employees will be able to work from home and work flexible hours rather than the standard 9 to 5. New mums will be able to share maternity leave with their partners – meaning that they can share 50 weeks off work between them. This will encourage more women into the workplace. The plans have been welcomed by unions but small businesses have warned of rising costs. Some small business owners have criticised the proposals saying that it will be impossible to coordinate employees in the workplace as staff come and go when they want.*

Health and safety
These laws look after the rights of the workforce in terms of their **wellbeing** in the workplace.
- A business has to provide the correct training to employees to ensure the job can be carried out safely
- Provide all necessary safety equipment and where appropriate safety clothing e.g. helmets or steel toe capped boots
- Responsible for ensuring standards are maintained by all employees
- Premises meet minimum standards e.g. toilets and washing facilities
- The work environment is safe e.g. fire exists are kept clear, warnings given near hazardous machines or chemicals and slippery services are identified

These laws **impact** on a small business because:
- Increased costs:
  - Wage costs may be higher
  - Additional expenses e.g. health and safety equipment and training
  - Ensuring premises are accessible to all e.g. lifts and ramps if necessary
- Could be taken to court if the laws are ignored and legal action taken:
  - Fined
  - Prosecuted including possible imprisonment
  - Closed down
- The reputation of the firm may suffer if the firm fails to follow the laws:
  - Bad publicity
  - Loss of customers
  - Difficult to recruit
- However they could help motivate workers who feel they are fairly treated and safe

People in Business – Test Yourself

4.1 Recruitment
1. Identify two reasons why a business may need to recruit.
2. Explain one benefit of full-time employment to a business.
3. Explain one benefit of part-time employment to a business.
4. Explain one benefit of internal recruitment.
5. Explain one benefit of external recruitment.
6. Identify and explain two methods a business may use to recruit employees.
7. Explain how a business decides on suitable remuneration for a new employee.
8. What are pension payments?
9. Explain why a bonus might motivate a worker.
10. Explain, with the use of an appropriate example, what is meant by a non-monetary reward.

4.2 Motivating Staff
1. Explain two benefits to a business of having well-motivated staff.
2. Explain how training might motivate staff.
3. Identify and explain one other method of motivating staff.
4. Why might the methods of motivation available to a small business be limited?

4.3 Protecting Staff through Understanding Legislation
1. What is equal pay?
2. Explain how the minimum wage law affects small businesses.
3. Identify two additional responsibilities an employer has towards its workforce.
4. Explain why it is important for a business to protect staff.

People in Business – Practice Questions

Read the item and then answer the questions that follow.
Total for this question: 23 marks

Item

Highly Strung
Marcello and Louis own a successful, small music shop. They stock a wide range of musical instruments and accessories. They have built a loyal customer base with repeat customers often asking to see Marcello or Louis in person for expert help. Marcello thinks they could offer two new services:
- Repairs and restringing
- Music tuition

They currently both work full-time in the business as well as employing 3 sales assistants. Two of the sales assistants are students at the local music college who work part-time in the shop. The third sales assistant is employed full-time. He works very hard but is frustrated as he feels the two students do not do their fair share of the work.

1. State two ways in which legislation helps to protect workers. (2 marks)
2. Marcello and Louis have decided to recruit a part-time music tutor.
   List two different ways in which they could advertise this vacancy. (2 marks)
3. Louis has suggested they appoint a sales manager.
   Explain one benefit and one drawback of recruiting externally. (4 marks)
4. Highly Strung has received 20 applicants for the job of sales manager.
   Explain how they could decide upon the best applicant for the job. (6 marks)
5. Explain one benefit to Highly Strung of employing both full-time and part-time workers. (4 marks)
6. Marcello and Louis are concerned about low levels of motivation affecting the level of service given to customers.
   - Louis has suggested employees are set targets for sales and paid a bonus if these are met
   - Marcello prefers the idea of giving each employee more responsibility with a pay review after six months

   Recommend which action Highly Strung should take in order to improve the level of service given to customers. Give reasons for your recommendation. (9 Marks)

Production Methods for Manufacturing & Providing Services

What do you need to know and understand?
- Job and batch production methods
- The importance to a business of operating efficiently
- The role of technology in achieving operational efficiency
- Customers' expectations of quality

Operations management is the management and coordination of resources to create a good or service.

Methods of production include:
Job production
The production of one off items to meet the needs of each individual customer.
- Cheap and easy to set up, but more expensive to produce
- Often a specialist service
- Time consuming to produce
- Meet specific needs of customers
- Examples include:
  - Tailor made clothes and jewellery
  - Specialist cakes
  - Web designs

Delicious chocolates for that special moment - *Natalie Allen founded Delicious Moments as she saw a gap in the market for a bespoke chocolate service. She produces a range of chocolates that can be customised according to customer tastes. Customers can order their own shapes, chocolate, fillings and even colours to match their special event such as weddings. The tailor made chocolates are produced using job production. Once Natalie has her customer's requirements she sets about producing outstanding chocolates tailored to the event. People are willing to pay high prices for this sort of premium product meaning that Delicious Moments can compete against lower priced, lower quality offerings.*
www.delicious-moments.co.uk

Batch Production
Identical items are produced in groups (batches), each item passing through the production process at the same time.
- Allows for cheaper and quicker production of items
- More uniform products
- Variation can be achieved in different batches
- If there is a fault the whole batch will be affected
- Examples include: Bread, Jeans, Garden furniture

Operational efficiency involves making the best use of **inputs** (resources) to achieve a given **output** (finished good).

A firm will try to be operationally efficient in order to increase the gap between the cost of the inputs and sales revenue received from the outputs. This could include:
- Better quality materials • Increased capacity • Lower wastage

A firm can increase efficiency through a number of methods including:
- Staff training • Improved procedures
- Specialisation • Reduced wastage
- Improved motivation • Increased use of **technology**

Efficiency and technology
Technology is the use of computers and machinery within the production process, it can play a major role in improving efficiency and reducing costs.

Technology	In operations management	Improved efficiency
Robots / automation	Machines rather than people to carry out tasks. Making the production process run automatically	Less human error. Increased output. Can operate 24/7
CAD/CAM	Computers to enhance design and manufacturing capabilities	Sophisticated design software. Simulate environments e.g. wind tunnels to improve design. Easy to make changes to designs
Computerised stock control	Monitoring of stock levels and automatically reordering when low. Use of bar codes and databases	Should never be short of stock due to human error. Can reduce stock holdings and save on costs. Do not hold too much stock that could lose value

However technology costs money. It may break down, staff will need training and it needs to be correctly set up in the first place!

Quality issues
Customers expect a good or service to meet certain standards.
This will include:
- Is it fit for the purpose that it was bought for?
- Does it at least meet minimum standards expected by customers?
- Does the customer believe that the product is worth the money paid?

Quality is important to a business because it:
- Helps build a reputation and gain customer loyalty
- Reduces complaints and returns
- Reduces waste from scrapping faulty products
- Gains positive word of mouth advertising e.g. customers tell a friend

Quality can be achieved through **quality control** i.e. checking of finished goods or **quality assurance** i.e. checking at each stage in the production process.

Customer Service

What do you need to know and understand?
- Importance of customer service to small businesses
- How customers are protected by law
- The impact of ICT developments on customer service

Importance of customer service
Customer service is the meeting of customer expectations before, during and after purchasing a good or service.
For a small business it is essential to have good customer service in order to:
- Distinguish the product from the competition • Obtain repeat custom
- Gain a good reputation

It is important to provide good customer service in a number of areas:

Reliability
- Customers want a product that will meet their requirements **each** and **every** time
- Delivered on time
- As described and fit for purpose

Product information
- To obtain the full benefit of a product the customer needs to know how it works
- Expert knowledge will allow the firm to help a customer make an informed decision
- Technical knowledge may require staff training

After sales service
- Many products require an ongoing service
- A good website, online helpdesk and a reliable repair/support team can provide this
- Continued high level of service to match the terms of any warranties or guarantees

It is in the interest of the business to provide a good level of customer service to protect their reputation. However not all firms do treat customers fairly. Therefore customers are also **protected by law**.
Examples of **consumer protection** include:
- All products sold must be as described e.g. if a scarf says 100% silk it must be 100% silk so as not to deceive the customer
- Products must be fit for purpose i.e. of a good enough standard e.g. wood glue must be able to hold two pieces of wood together securely
- Food products must be safe for customers to eat and list all the ingredients accurately
- Quantities stated on packaging must be accurate e.g. a pint of milk can not be less than a pint

At fresh food chain Pret a Manger staff are monitored to make sure they are "relentlessly cheerful" when dealing with customers. Mystery shoppers visit stores every week to check that all staff are displaying 'Pret perfect' behaviour. The business says that all staff must be 'charming', 'have presence' and create a 'sense of fun'. Workers should not 'annoy people' or be 'moody' or 'bad-tempered'. If the mystery shopper gives a branch a positive report the whole team gets a bonus. If the report is bad the whole team misses out on the bonus.

Impact of ICT on customer service

Advances in ICT have allowed customer services to develop. This has been made possible through:

Websites
These allow consumers to access a firm's products through the Internet
- They are cheap and easy for a firm to set up
- They allow the consumer to identify and purchase products, read product information and reviews
- Provision for after sales service with extensive information accessible to customers
- Online live chat help lines • Blogs sharing reviews
- Frequently asked questions • Support available 24/7

E-commerce

- Electronic commerce is any form of business transaction between the firm and a consumer through the use of ICT e.g. online shopping
- The Internet allows access to customers 24 hours, 7 days a week
- E-commerce improves the speed of sales
- Small firms can source cheaper supplies through the Internet
- Customers can easily compare product details AND prices
- Easy and safe payment methods

Global/International markets
- ICT has opened up a global economy for small firms
- Small firms no longer have to remain in local or regional markets
- ICT will help to improve customer service through quicker response times e.g. an e-mail takes no longer to reach Australia than somewhere in the UK
- Customers can easily find products from anywhere in the world
- Offer cheap alternatives to expensive high street shops
- Increased variety

How would you prefer to receive customer help:
• in person • over the phone • online?

Operations Management – Test Yourself

5.1 Production Methods for Manufacturing and Providing a Service
1. What is job production?
2. What is batch production?
3. State and explain one example where job production is appropriate.
4. State and explain one example where batch production is appropriate.
5. Explain two benefits to a business of operating efficiently.
6. Explain how technology can be used to increase operational efficiency.
7. What is quality?
8. Explain the benefits to a business of meeting customer expectations.

5.2 Customer Service
1. Explain the importance of each of the following aspects of customer service:
   a. Reliability
   b. Product information
   c. Good after sales service
2. Explain two ways in which consumers are protected by law.
3. Explain two ways in which ICT has helped customer service develop.

Operations Management – Practice Questions

Read the item and then answer the questions that follow.
Total for this question: 21 marks

Item

Pick a Perfect Pizza
Tim and Leo run Perfect Pizza, a popular pizza takeaway, in the busy business district of Bristol. They pride themselves on their excellent reputation and unique service. The pizza bases are made in the morning using batch production but then each individual pizza is completed to the exact requirements of the customer.

Customers can choose their base type, sauce, toppings and even the type of cheese. This makes the shop very popular with lots of repeat customers. However as the business has become more established they now struggle to meet demand during the lunch time rush when office workers pile in. Taking each order and making the pizzas to meet the customer's exact requirements takes time. On some days the queue is out the door and customers start to complain that they only have a short lunch break.

1. State two features of batch production. (2 marks)
2. Explain one benefit to Perfect Pizza of using job production for making their pizzas. (3 marks)
3. Tim and Leo pride themselves on their excellent reputation.
   Explain two benefits to Perfect Pizza of an excellent reputation. (4 marks)
4. Explain one way in which Perfect Pizza will be affected by consumer protection. (3 marks)
5. Tim and Leo are concerned about an increasing number of complaints as a result of long queues. They are considering either:
   - Offering standardised toppings so that pizzas can be prepared in advance
   - Introducing an online ordering system so customers can pre-order an hour in advance and then collect

   Recommend which action the business should take in order to ensure continued customer satisfaction. Give reasons for your recommendation. (9 marks)

Exam Technique

About your exam

How long is the exam?	1 Hour
How many marks is it out of?	60 marks
What does this mean?	You have roughly 1 minute writing time for each mark (well slightly less really because you also need to read the items!)
What will the exam look like?	3 items each followed with a range of questions that get more difficult. You must try to answer all of the questions – so manage your time carefully.
What will you need?	Black ink or ball-point pen and a calculator.

What types of questions will you get?

Command word (this is the examiner giving you an instruction.)	What must you do?
State	Simply show off your business knowledge. Give a relevant point e.g. **State two** ways in which laws help to protect workers. • 1 Health and safety • 2 Minimum wage There is **no** need to spend time giving any more detail.
State and Explain **Explain**	State a relevant point and then say **why** your point is of importance or relevant to the business in the item. One way to do this is to say what it has meant for the business e.g. more customers, better reputation, ability to save money. e.g. Explain one benefit to Perfect Pizza of using job production for making their pizzas. (3 marks) - page 43 qu b Job production will allow Perfect Pizza to make each pizza to meet the customers needs (relevant point). This is important because it makes the business have a unique service (from item/ in context). Which has led to the business being very busy with an excellent reputation. Make a point, link to the item, say why important or what effect has been.
Advice – Give reasons for your advice **Recommend – Give reasons for your recommendation**	The big (9) mark questions. You need to think about your answer – don't jump straight in! • First think carefully about the options and weigh them up in the context of the case • Ask yourself why is your point an argument for or against each option • What is your recommendation going to be? Now you will be ready to write a well thought out answer.

Exam Technique

Pick a Perfect Pizza (page 43)

Tim and Leo are concerned about an increasing number of complaints as a result of long queues. They are considering either:
- Offering standardised toppings so that pizzas can be prepared in advance
- Introducing an online ordering system so that customers can pre-order an hour in advance and then collect

Recommend which action the business should take in order to ensure continued customer satisfaction. Give reasons for your recommendation. (9 marks)

Mark Scheme

This is what the examiner is looking at when they read your answer and decide what mark to give you.

Level	Descriptor	Marks	Assessment Objective
1	State relevant points	1	AO1 (Knowledge only)
0	No valid response	0	
2	Describes option(s) in the context of Perfect Pizza	2	AO2 (Application – uses item/ answers in context)
3	Analyses option(s) in the context of Perfect Pizza	4–3	AO3 (Analysis – explains why or cause and effect in context)

Lets ignore the bottom 2 levels and aim high. Both of these say in context i.e. **USE THE ITEM**

Have you spotted anything?

The question is out of 9 – so where do the other 5 marks come from?
Answer – the ability to make reasoned judgements and present a justified conclusion i.e.
- Make and fully justify a recommendation about which option is best
- Offer and fully justify advise about which option is best
- Best for who?
- **THE BUSINESS IN THE ITEM**

Think about it!

If the question is out of 9 and 5 marks are for your conclusion which part of your answer is the most important?
Too many students spend too long weighing up (discussing) the advantages and disadvantages without giving sufficient time to their conclusion.

Make your answer stand out from the crowd!

Just a suggestion:

Step 1: Make a decision e.g. introducing an online ordering system is the best option
Step 2: Now write a paragraph explaining the benefits to Perfect Pizza of an online system
Step 3: Now write a paragraph explaining the drawbacks of standardised toppings
You now have time to dedicate to your conclusion
Step 4: Recommend online system – justify in terms of how this will help Perfect Pizza ensure continued customer satisfaction

See CD for model answer

GCSE Business Studies Unit 1

Index

Advertising 5, 19, 31, 34, 39
Bank loan 22
Batch production 38
Budget 16, 17, 19
Business aims 6
Business objectives 6, 7
Business plans 8, 9
Cash flow problems 27
Cash flow statements 26
Cash inflow 26
Cash outflows 26
Closing balance 26
Consumer protection 40
Competition 9, 13, 19, 40
Competitive market 19
Costs 5, 6, 8, 9, 12, 13, 19, 22, 24, 25, 27, 30, 31, 32, 34, 35, 39
Customer feedback 17
Customer satisfaction 6, 7, 45
Customer service 16, 25, 40, 41
Demand 13, 16, 19, 22, 30, 31
E-commerce 19, 41
Employment rights 34, 35
Enterprise 4, 7,
Entrepreneur 4, 5, 9, 17, 18, 23,
Equal pay 34
External recruitment 30
Financial rewards 35
Focus groups 17
Franchise 4, 5,
Franchisee 5
Franchisor 5
Full-time employee 30

Grants 22, 23
Growth 6, 7, 11
Health and safety 35, 44
International markets 19, 41
Internal recruitment 30
Internet research 17
Interview 31
Labour 12
Job production 38, 44
Legal structure 9, 10, 23
Legislation 34
Limited liability 10, 11
Loss 8, 9, 11, 24, 25, 33, 35
Market 4, 5, 6, 7, 8, 9, 13, 16, 17, 18, 19, 23, 25,
38, 41
Market niche 4, 5,
Market share 6, 7
Market research 5, 9, 16, 17, 19
Marketing activities 18
Marketing mix 9, 16, 18, 19
Minimum wage 34, 44
Monetary benefits 31
Mortgage 22, 23
Motivation 32, 39
Net cash flow 26
Non-monetary benefits 31
Operational efficiency 38
Overdraft 22, 27
Partnership 10
Part-time employee 30
Personal recommendations 19
Place 9, 13, 16, 18, 19
Price 9, 18, 19, 24, 25

Product 4, 5, 12, 16, 17, 18,
19, 25, 32, 33, 38, 39,
40, 41
Profit 5, 6, 7, 8, 9, 11, 16,
24, 25, 32, 33
Promotion 5, 9, 18, 19, 25,
30, 31, 33
Quality 5, 6, 9, 12, 13, 19,
25, 27, 30, 32, 33, 38,
39
Questionnaires 17
Raising finance 8, 23
Raw materials 12, 13, 25,
26
Receivership 27
Recruitment 30, 31, 32, 34
Remuneration 30, 31
Responsibility 33
Revenue 19, 24, 25, 39
Risk 5, 8, 9, 10, 11, 22, 23
Sales 6, 7, 13, 16, 18, 19,
24, 26, 39, 40
Shareholders 7, 11
SMART objectives 9
Social enterprise 4, 23
Sole trader 10
Sources of finance 9, 22,
Stakeholders 6, 7, 10, 11,
13
Supplier feedback 17
Surveys 17
Survival 6, 7
Technology 13, 25, 38, 39
Training 30, 32, 33, 35,
39, 40
Transport 12, 13, 25
Unlimited liability 10, 11